easy GUITAR TAB EDITION

HARD ROCK HITS
FOR EASY GUITAR

Alfred Publishing Co., Inc.
16320 Roscoe Blvd., Suite 100
P.O. Box 10003
Van Nuys, CA 91410-0003
alfred.com

ISBN-10: 0-7390-4206-8
ISBN-13: 978-0-7390-4206-9

CONTENTS

BAD COMPANY

*To match record key, tune guitar down one half step.

Words and Music by
PAUL RODGERS and MICK RALPHS

ALL ALONG THE WATCHTOWER

*To match record key, tune guitar down one half step.

Words and Music by
BOB DYLAN

1. "There must be some kind of way out of here," said the jok-er to the thief.__
2. "No rea-son to get ex-cit-ed," the thief, he kind-ly spoke.
3. *See additional lyrics*

"There's too much con-fu-sion, I can't get no re-lief.__
"There are man-y here a-mong us who feel that life is but a joke,__ but,

All Along the Watchtower - 2 - 1
25812

Verse 3:
All along the watchtower,
Princes kept the view.
While all the women came and went,
Barefoot servants, too.
Well, outside in the cold distance,
A wild cat did growl.
Two riders were approaching
And the wind began to howl.
(To Outro:)

DR. FEELGOOD

*To match record key, tune guitar down one whole step.

Music by MICK MARS and NIKKI SIXX
Lyrics by NIKKI SIXX

Moderate shuffle ♩ = 102
N.C. (E5)

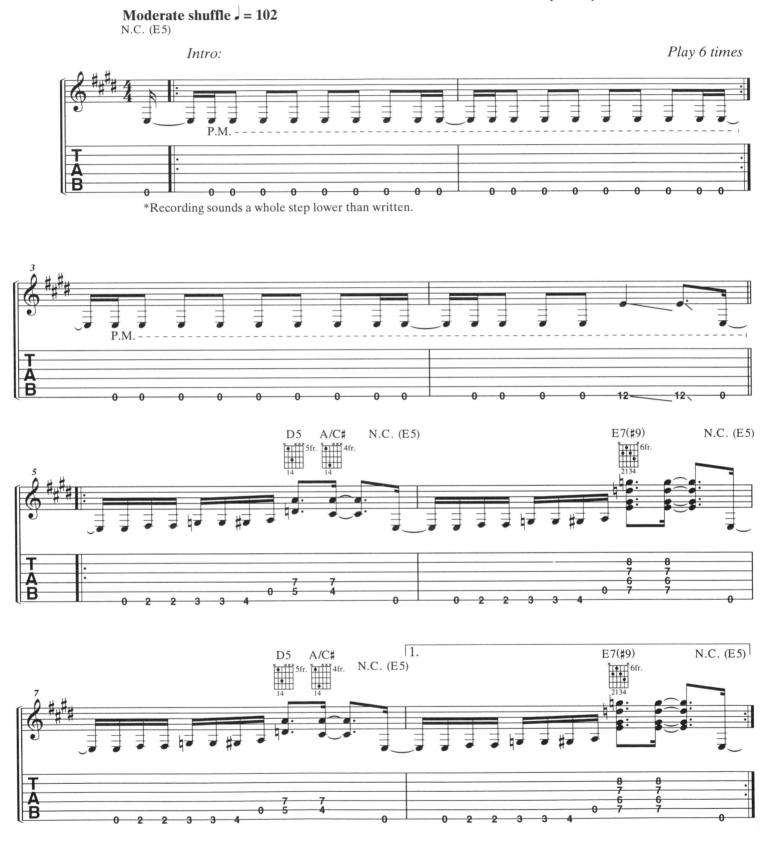

*Recording sounds a whole step lower than written.

Chorus:

pack-ag-es of can-dy-cane.___ He's___ the one they call Doc-tor Feel - good.___ He's___

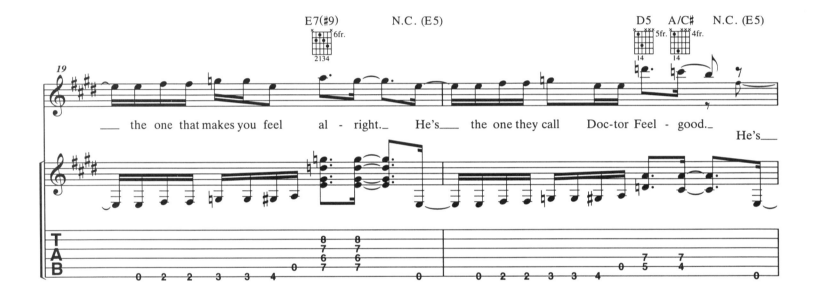

___ the one that makes you feel al - right.___ He's___ the one they call Doc-tor Feel - good.___ He's___

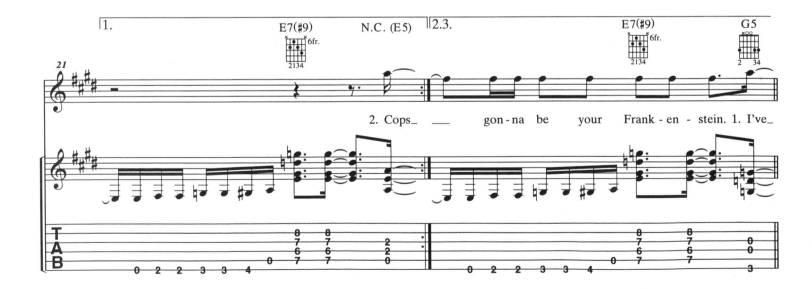

2. Cops___ ___ gon-na be your Frank-en - stein. 1. I've___

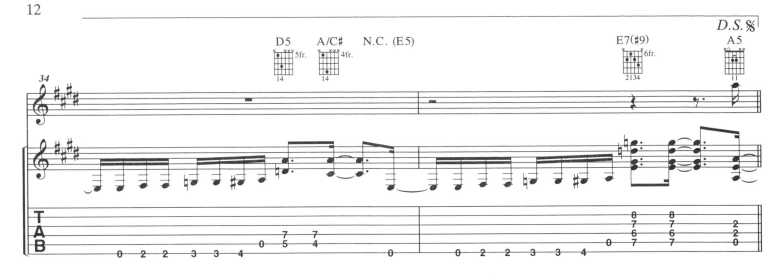

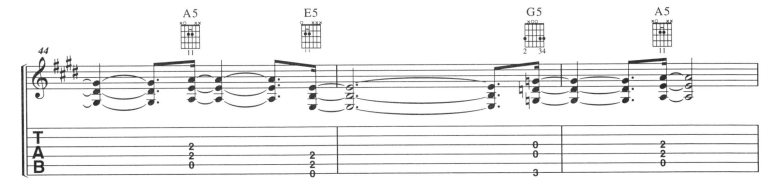

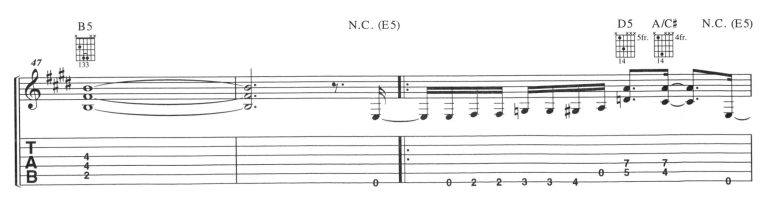

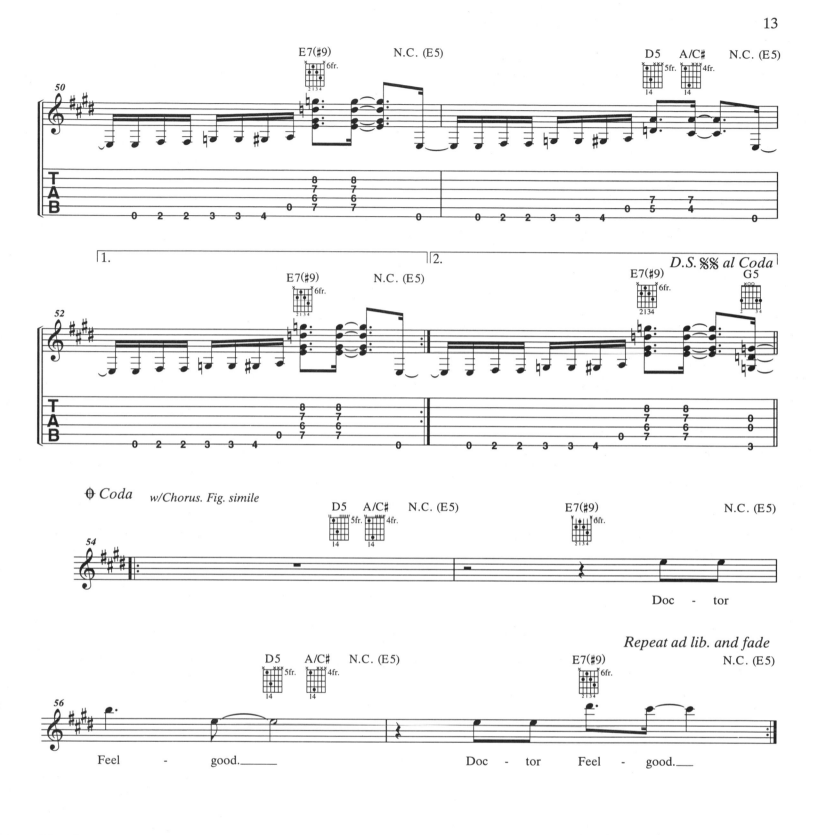

Verse 2:
Cops on the corner always ignore.
Somebody's getting paid.
Jimmy's got it wired, law's for hire;
Got it made in the shade.
Got a little hide-away,
Does his business all day,
But at night he'll always be found
Selling sugar to the sweet people on the street.
Call this Jimmy's town.
(To Chorus:)

Verse 3:
He'll tell you he's the king of these barrio streets
Moving up to Shangri-La.
Came by his wealth as a matter of luck.
Says he never broke the law.
Two-time loser, running out of juice,
Time to move out quick.
Heard a rumor goin' 'round,
Jimmy's goin' down.
This time it's gonna stick.
(To Chorus:)

Bridge 2:
Let him soothe your soul,
Just take his hand.
Some people call him an evil man.
Let him introduce himself real good.
He's the only one they call "Feel-good."
(To Guitar Solo:)

DIRTY DEEDS DONE DIRT CHEAP

Words and Music by
ANGUS YOUNG, MALCOLM YOUNG
and BON SCOTT

1. If you're

Verse:

hav-ing trou-ble with the high-school head,
2. You got prob-lems in your life of love,
3. *See additional lyrics*

he's giv-ing you the blues.
you got a bro-ken heart.

Cont. rhy. simile

You wan-na grad-u-ate but not in his bed,
He's dou-ble deal-ing with your best friend,

here's what you got-ta do.
that's when the tear-drops start, fel-la.

Pick up the phone, I'm al-ways home.
Pick up the phone, I'm here a-lone

Call me an-y-time.
or make a so-cial call.

Just ring

three, six, two, four, three, six, oh.
Come right in, for-get a-bout him

I lead a life of crime.
we'll have our-selves a ball.

Dirty Deeds Done Dirt Cheap - 3 - 1
25812

Verse 3:
If you got a lady and you want her gone,
But you ain't got the guts.
She keeps nagging you night and day,
Enough to drive you nuts.
(To Chorus:)

FEEL LIKE MAKIN' LOVE

All gtrs. in Drop D tuning:
⑥ = D   ③ = G
⑤ = A   ② = B
④ = D   ① = E

Words and Music by
PAUL RODGERS and MICK RALPHS

Chorus:

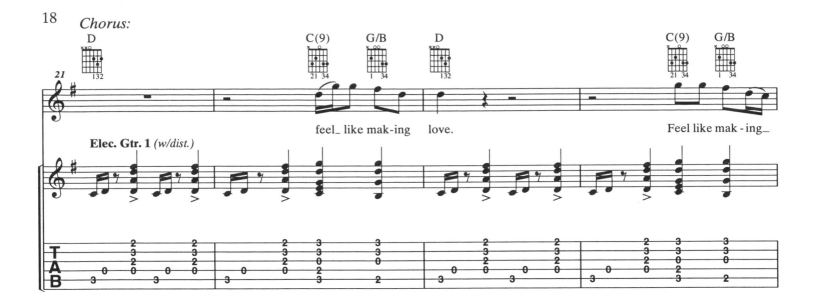

feel_ like mak-ing love.

Feel like mak-ing_

love.

Feel like mak - ing_ love.

Feel like

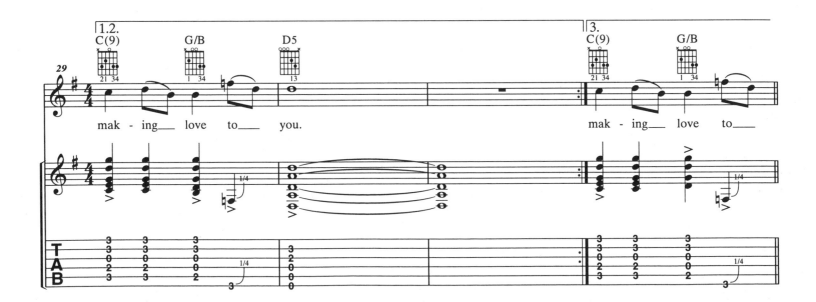

mak - ing_ love to_ you.

mak-ing_ love to_

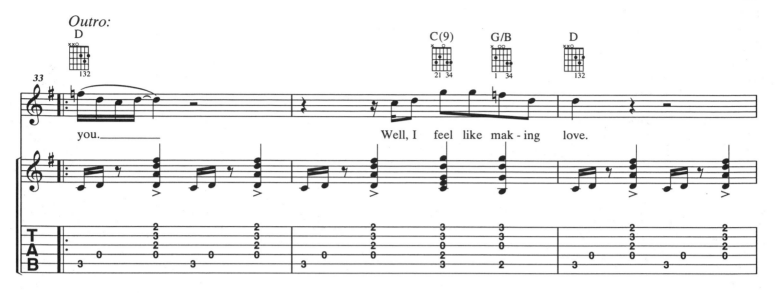

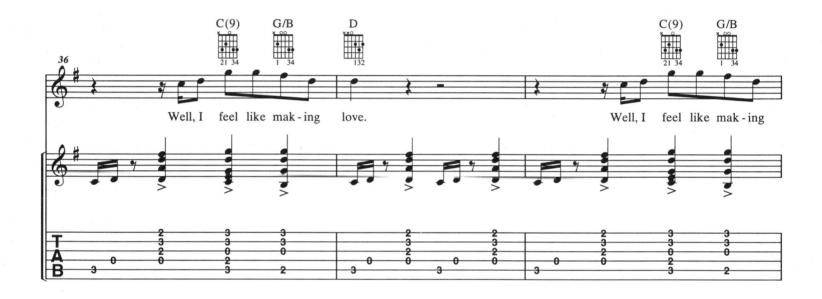

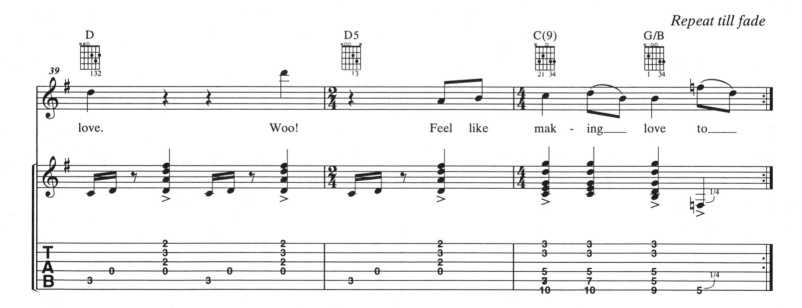

IN-A-GADDA-DA-VIDA

Words and Music by
DOUG INGLE

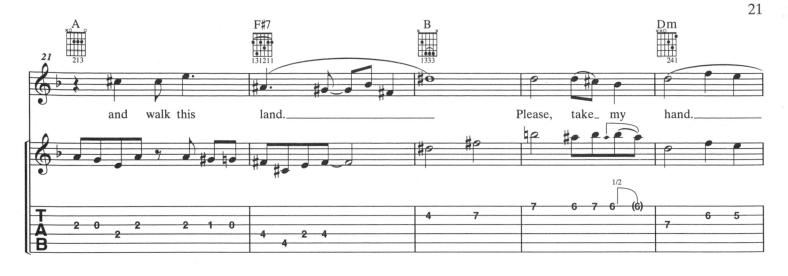

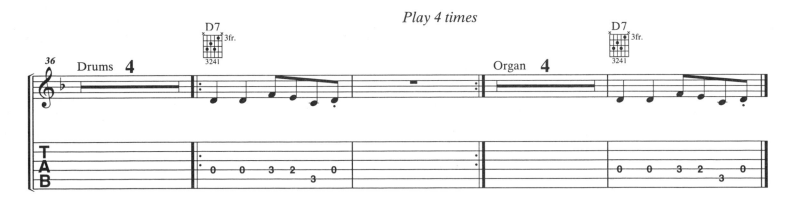

ROCK & ROLL BAND

Words and Music by
TOM SCHOLZ

Rock & Roll Band - 4 - 1
25812

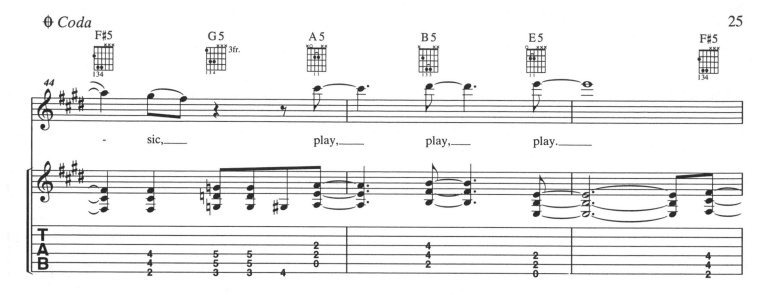

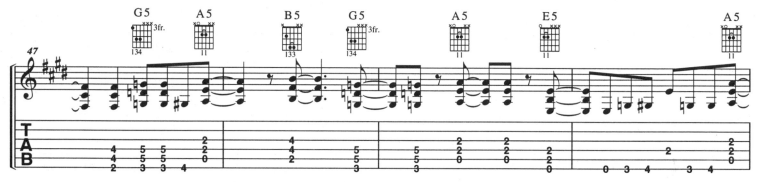

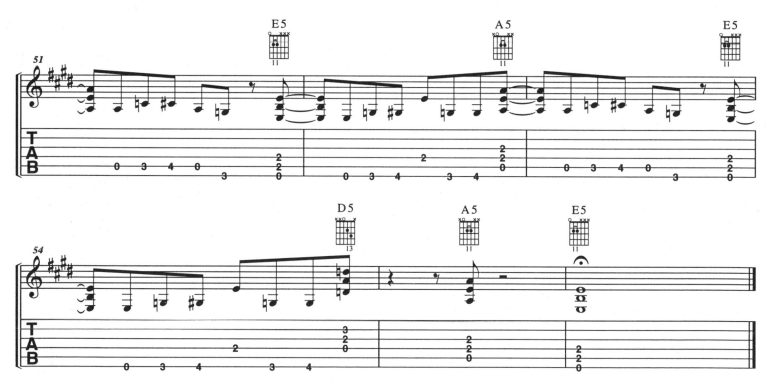

Verse 3:
Playin' for a week in Rhode Island;
A man came to the stage one night.
He smoked a big cigar
And drove a Cadillac car
And said, "Boys, I think this band's outta sight.
Sign a record company contract,
You know I've got great expectations.
When I hear you on the car radio,
You're gonna to be a sensation."
(To Chorus:)

PANAMA

*To match record key, tune guitar down one half step.

Words and Music by
EDWARD VAN HALEN, ALEX VAN HALEN
and DAVID LEE ROTH

Moderate rock ♩ = 144

Intro:

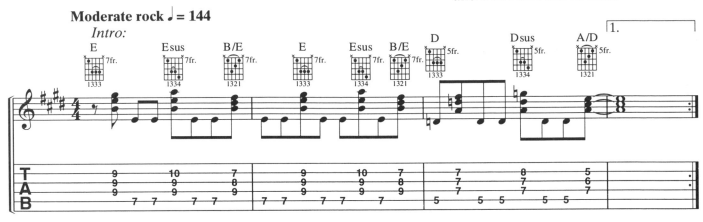

*Recording sounds a half step lower than written.

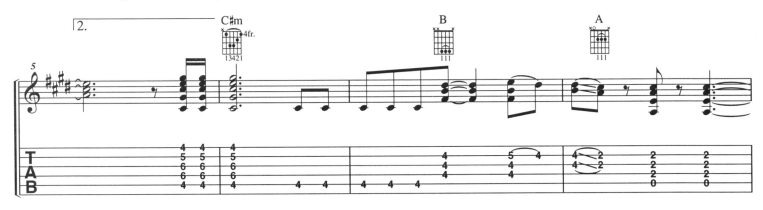

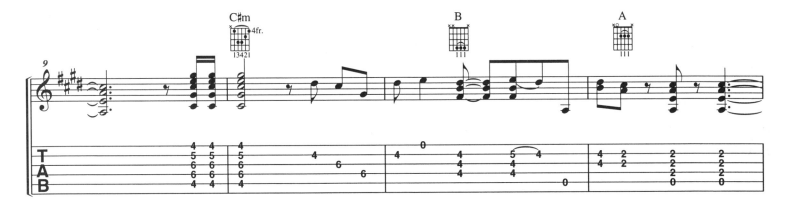

Panama - 5 - 1
25812

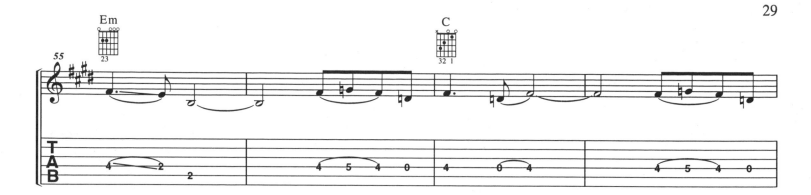

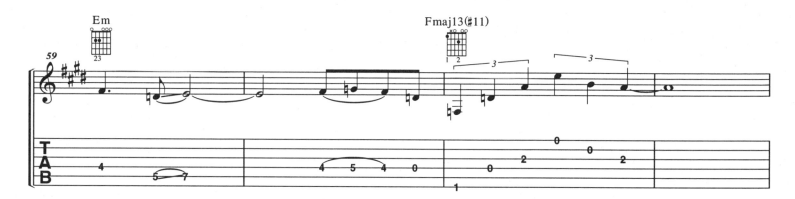

Bridge:

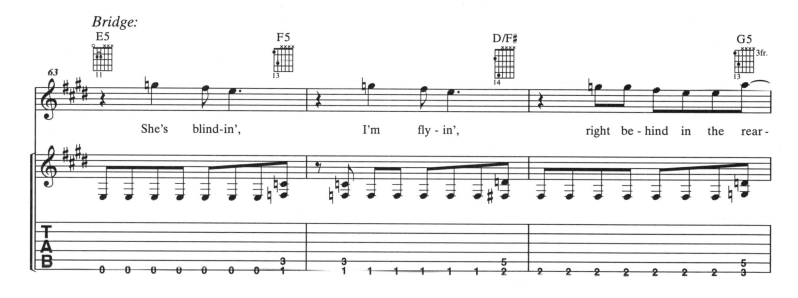

She's blind-in', I'm fly-in', right be-hind in the rear-

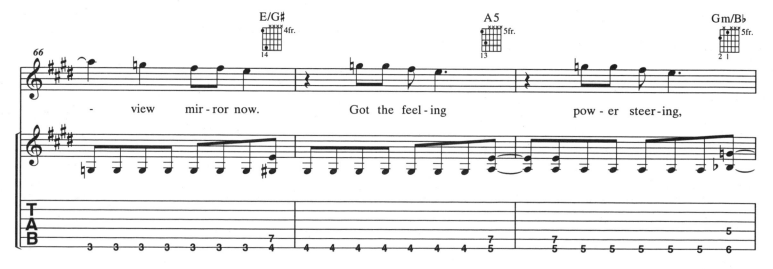

-view mir-ror now. Got the feel-ing pow-er steer-ing,

Panama - 5 - 4
25812

Verse 2:
Ain't nothin' like it, her shiny machine,
Got the feel for the wheel, keep the moving parts clean.
Hot shoe, burnin' down the avenue,
Got an on ramp comin' through my bedroom.
Don't you know she's comin' home to me?
You'll lose her in the turn.
I'll get her!
(To Chorus:)

RUNNIN' WITH THE DEVIL

*To match record key, tune guitar down one half step.

Words and Music by
EDWARD VAN HALEN, ALEX VAN HALEN,
MICHAEL ANTHONY and DAVID LEE ROTH

*Recording sounds a half step lower than written.

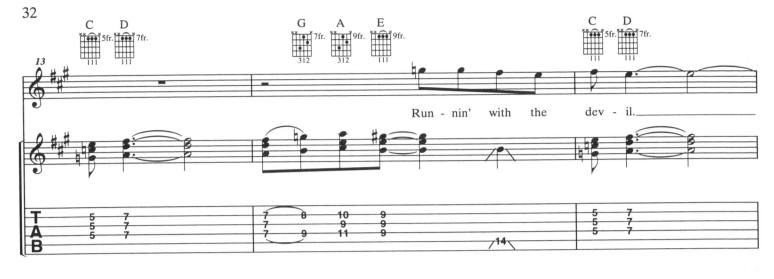

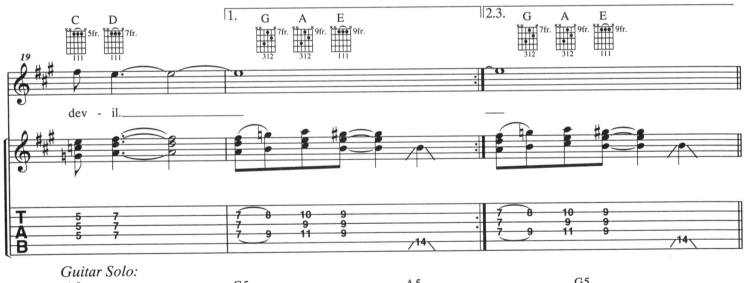

Guitar Solo:

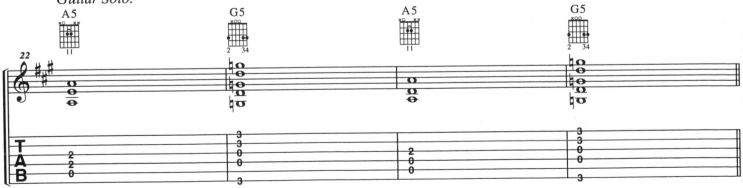

Verse 2:
I found the simple life ain't so simple
When I jumped out on that road.
I got no love, no love you'd call real.
Ain't got nobody waiting at home.
(To Chorus:)

Verse 3:
I found the simple life weren't so simple, no
When I jumped out on that road.
Got no love, no love you'd call real.
Got nobody waiting at home.
(To Chorus:)

SHOOTING STAR

Words and Music by
PAUL RODGERS

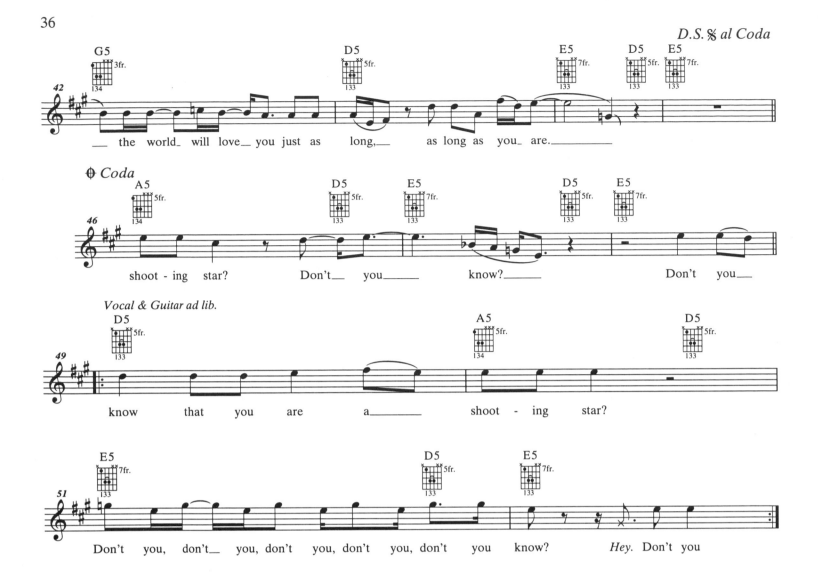

Verse 3:
Johnny made a record,
Went straight up to number one.
Suddenly everyone loved to hear him sing the song.
Watching the world go by,
Surprising it goes so fast.
Johnny looked around him and said,
"Well, I made the big name at last."
Don't you know?
Don't you know?
(To Chorus:)

Verse 4:
Johnny died one night,
Died in his bed.
Bottle of whiskey, sleeping tablets by his head.
Johnny's life passed him by
Like a warm summer day.
If you listen to the wind, you can
Still hear him play.
Oh, oh.
(To Chorus:)

SPOONFUL

Written by
WILLIE DIXON

Moderate shuffle ♩ = 102

Intro:
E7(♯9)

1. Could fill a spoon's full of dia-monds,
2.3. *See additional lyrics*

could fill a spoon's full of gold.___ Just a___ lit-tle spoon of your___

For additional information on the genre of the blues please contact:
The Blues Heaven Foundation (Founded by Willie Dixon in 1981)
2120 S. Michigan Avenue, Chicago, IL 60616, (312) 808-1286 www.bluesheaven.com

precious love____ sat - is - fy____ my soul._____ Men____

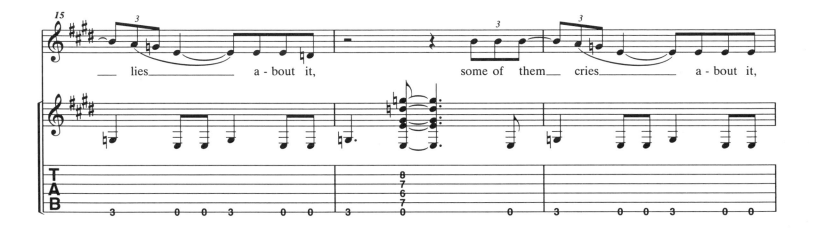

____ lies_____ a - bout it,   some of them____ cries_____ a - bout it,

some of them____ dies_____ a - bout it.   Ev -

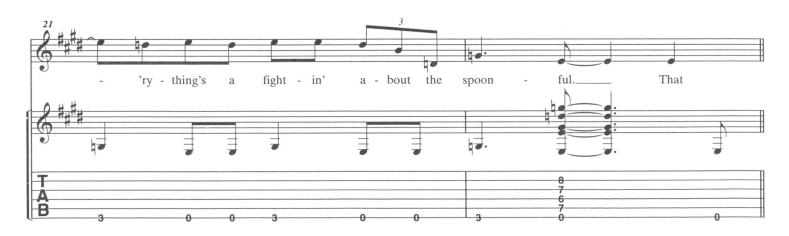

- 'ry - thing's a fight - in' a - bout the spoon - ful._____ That

Verse 2:
Could fill a spoonful of coffee; it could fill a spoonful of tea.
Just a little spoonful of your precious love is good enough for me.
Men lies about it.
Some of them cries about it.
Some of them dies about it.
Ev'rybody a-fightin' about the spoonful.
(To Chorus:)

Verse 3:
Could fill a spoonful of water; save it from the desert sand.
One little spoon of lead from my forty-five
Save you from another man.
Men lies about it.
Some of them cries about it.
Some of them dies about it.
Ev'rybody a-fightin' about the spoonful.
(To Chorus:)

WELCOME TO THE JUNGLE

*To match record key, tune guitar down one half step.

Words and Music by
W. AXL ROSE, SLASH, IZZY STRADLIN',
DUFF McKAGAN and STEVEN ADLER

Moderate rock ♩ = 104
Intro:

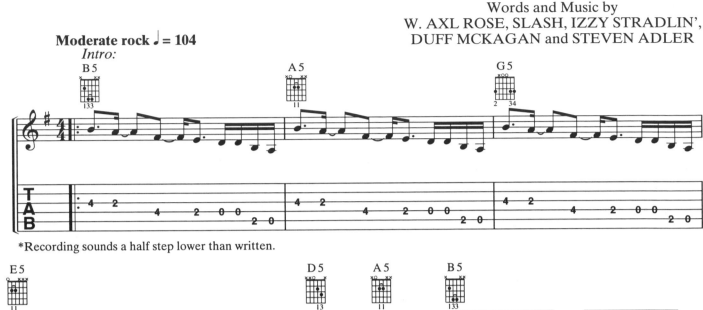

*Recording sounds a half step lower than written.

1. Wel-come to the jun - gle,   we got fun 'n' games..   We got ev-'ry-thing_ you want,_
2.3. *See additional lyrics*

Welcome to the Jungle - 6 - 1
25812

42

Interlude:

D.S. % al Coda

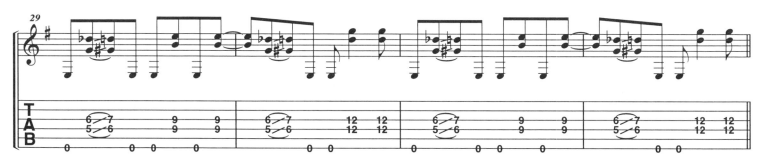

⊕ Coda

Bridge:

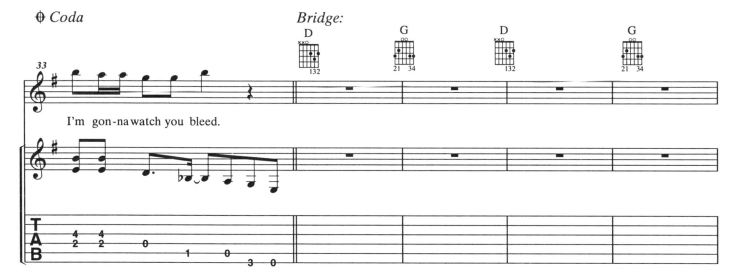

I'm gon-na watch you bleed.

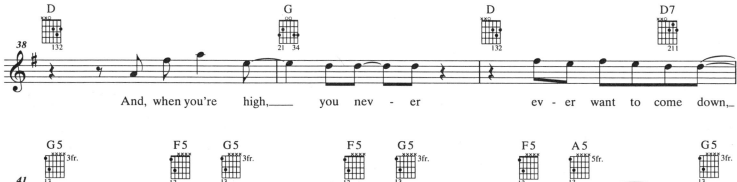

And, when you're high,___ you nev - er ev - er want to come down,_

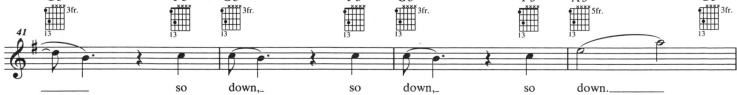

___ so down,_ so down,_ so down.___

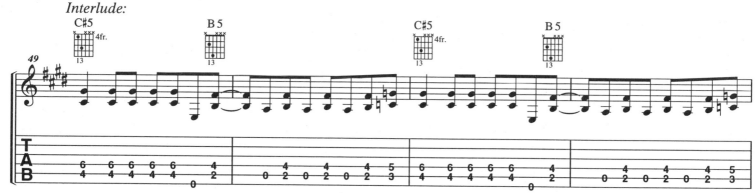

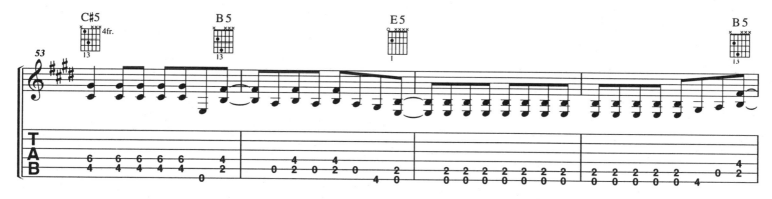

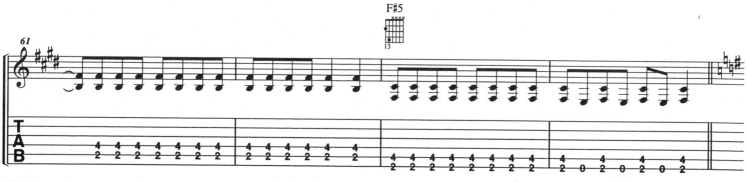

Welcome to the Jungle - 6 - 4
25812

Verse 2:
Welcome to the jungle,
We take it day by day.
If you want it, you're gonna bleed
But it's the price you pay.
And you're a very sexy girl
Who's very hard to please.
You can taste the bright lights
But you won't get them for free.
In the jungle,
Welcome to the jungle.
Feel my, my, my, my serpentine.
Uh, ah I wanna hear you scream!
(To Interlude:)

Verse 3:
Welcome to the jungle,
It gets worse every day.
You learn to live like an animal,
In the jungle where we play.
If you got a hunger for what you see,
You'll take it eventually.
You can have anything you want,
But you better not take it from me.
In the jungle,
Welcome to the jungle.
Watch it bring you to your
Sha na na na na na na na na na na na na
Knees, knees.
Uh. I'm gonna watch you bleed.
(To Bridge:)

SUNSHINE OF YOUR LOVE

Words and Music by
JACK BRUCE, PETE BROWN
and ERIC CLAPTON